Children of
the Third Reich

Children of the Third Reich

PAUL GARSON

AMBERLEY

First published 2019

Amberley Publishing
The Hill, Stroud
Gloucestershire, GL5 4EP

www.amberley-books.com

British Library Cataloguing in Publication Data.
A catalogue record for this book is available from the British Library.

ISBN 978 1 4456 9008 7 (print)
ISBN 978 1 4456 9009 4 (ebook)

Typesetting by Aura Technology and Software Services, India.
Printed in the Great Britain.

Strike First
Members of a German youth troop, with the help of a farmer, stretch one of their number over the chopping log, axes raised in mock murder.

The Images

The images that follow are sourced from the author's extensive collections of original photographs, postcards and documents collected over a period of many years from some twenty countries. While some were produced by commercial enterprises or Nazi State-run organisations, most were taken by the personal cameras of German soldiers and civilians that lived, fought and often died in the service of the Third Reich's twelve-year rule. Many began their baptism of fire in Nazi Germany's youth organisations where individual conscience was forcibly excised in the name of one overriding mindset, unquestioning obedience to the Führer and his mandates, and which eventually brought unprecedented ruin and destruction to much of Europe and to Germany instelf.

Introduction

Following Germany's defeat in the First World War and the subsequent political and economic turmoil, the country fell under the sway of the Nazi Party, which would take full advantage of the country's pre-existing and popular youth groups. The goal: to re-mould them by teaching an all-pervasive martial mindset based on unwavering uniformity of thought and action permeated by intense ultranationalism, virulent racism and anti-demoncratic fascist ideology. The purpose: to forge a new Germany from blood and iron, which was destined to rule Europe.

Italian Blackshirt Youth Take Part in 'The March on Rome', Signaling Mussolini's Rise to Power, 1922
It should be kept in historical context that Nazi Germany's blueprint for indoctrinating its youth was directly traceable to the Italian model for producing their 'citizen warrior'. The first formations of Fascist Youth began as early as 1919 with a focus on physical fitness, preliminary military training, discipline and political orientation, although devoid of the Nazi racist virulence. Many of the educational programmes were actually more advanced than later German ones.

Bolt-action Beginnings

Initial Italian youth training began at eighteen months through eight years with the so-called Children-of-the-She-Wolf sections. Various organisations were specifically developed for children from birth to eight, eight to eleven; eleven to fourteen; fourteen to sixteen; and sixteen to eighteen-year-old boys, bearing such labels as Musketeers and Vanguards. Girls' training began, as with the boys, from birth to eight; eight to fourteen (the latter 'Little Italians Feminine Gender'); and fourteen to eighteen ('Young Italians Feminine Gender'). By October 1930 all eighteen to twenty year olds were integrated into the Groups of Young Combatants (FGC) and by 1940 5 million were members of the Fascist Youth. In addition, youth groups of indigenous colonial countries were also formed, including those in Albania, Libya (Arab Youth), Eritrea, Ethiopia, East African and Mediterranean occupied areas.

One of the early battle cries of the Nazi Party was 'Make Way, you Old Ones!'. The Nazi movment seemed geared to bringing youth to a position of dominance, sweeping away the obsolete and old-fashioned and replacing it with a new religious fervor where only the fittest deserved to survive, and there were none more fit than the Aryan German *Ubermensch*.

As a result of the Nazi takeover and the implementation of its ruthless social engineering, all those born between 1916 and 1934 were destined to be absorbed into the 'Hitler Youth' generation and conditioned to be the forbearers of the Thousand-Year Reich.

The term Hitler Youth (*Hitler-Jugend*) came into official use in July 1926 when German youth groups were placed under the control of the SA and divided into several geographic areas, or *Obergebeite*, specifically *Nord, Sud, West, Ost, Mitte* and *Sudost*.

By 1936 the *Hitler-Jugend* would count 5.4 million members aged ten to eighteen. Almost all pre-Third Reich youth groups, both for boys and girls, were assimilated into the Nazi collective organisations.

Some groups balked, particularly the religously affiliated, but all eventually fell under the thrall of the State, whose control and conditioning of Germany's children was a top priority. The State would supplant the traditional family as the controlling force.

Hitler Youth for boys was divided into sections based on age: the so-called 'Little Fellows', known as *Pimpf* recruited six to ten year olds; the *Deutsche Jungvolk* (German Young People) required the age of ten to thirteen for admittance and had a focus on paramilitary training. Members transferred at fourteen to the regular Hitler Youth, remaining there through to the age of eighteen, during which time they received more martial training, before transitioning to their civilian labour service via RAD (*Reichsartbeitdienst*), and finally on to military service in the Wehrmacht (army, navy, air force or SS). For girls aged fourteen to eighteen they joined the *Jungmadel* (Young Maidens) with training emphasising healthy habits, duties of the housewife and child-raising. Emphasis was also placed on Nazi racial dictums inflamed by its anti-Jewish virulence. Between fourteen and twenty-one, girls took part in further State-sponsored motherhood training via the BdM (*Bund Deutsche Madel*), or League of German Maidens.

Motherhood was sacrosanct in Nazi Germany, with mothers being assured they were ranked with the same status of front-line troops. A popular slogan was 'I have given a soldier to the Führer'. In effect, they were the breeding ground for the replenishment of the fallen warriors of the Fatherland. Prolific childbearers were awarded special medals: the Honor Cross of the German Mother, which was awarded in bronze for more than four children, silver for more than six and gold for more than eight. Hitler

Youth members were required to salute any woman wearing the award. In seeking to fill the ranks lost during the First World War and the mounting casualties on the new war's battlefields, the Third Reich encouraged high birth rates via various incentives, including financial inducements. During December 1939, four months into the war, and May 1940, the invasion of France, some 121,853 gold medals were awarded.

> I want a brutal, domineering, fearless, cruel youth. Youth must be all that. It must bear pain. There must be nothing weak and gentle about it. The free, splendid beast of prey must once again flash from its eyes. That is how I will eradicate thousands of years of human domestication. That is how I will create the New Order.
>
> Adolf Hitler

From cradle to grave, Nazi propaganda bombarded children with images romanticising war and exalting a glorious death for the Führer and Fatherland. The basic Hitler Youth ideology, besides echoing the Nazi world view and indoctrination, trumpeted opposition to that which it deemed 'decadent', including American-style films, jazz and modern international art forms. Much of its activities focused on outdoor life and physical exercise with an emphasis on militarisation via socialisation. Additionally, some Hitler Youth were given special training at concentration camps.

An estimated 1.5 million Hitler Youth boys received paramilitary training, including the use of the rifle. 50,000 boys would earn the marksmanship medal, which indicated their proficiency at accurate firing to a distance of 50 meters (164 feet). By 1936, some 2 million girls belonged to the BdM under the direction of some 125,000 BdM leaders, who saw to their training at thirty-five area schools. Evidence of the intensity of the indoctrination programme can be seen in the use of some 200,000 special trains required to transport 5 million German youth to the 12,000 Hitler Youth camps during the reign of the Third Reich.

In 1939 the State had mandated Hitler Youth membership for all boys and girls and as a result could count 7 million recruited, or nearly 82 per cent of eligible German youth enrolled. Further decrees made it mandatory for the remaining hold-outs to join or suffer the consequences. In 1945, with 8 million in the Hitler Youth, and during the last weeks of the war, boys and girls as young as ten would be manning anti-aircraft guns or were being sent against the Russian and American forces, some riding bicycles mounted with grenade launchers.

Educational System Supplanted by Ideology

The cover blurb for one of the Nazi-authorised school textbooks proclaimed: 'Who wants to live has to fight, and whoever refuses to fight in this world of eternal challenge has no right to live.'

Usurping the role of the traditional German school system was a priority for the Nazi State, eased by the fact that it was already traditionally a very conservative system. Hitler himself credited an early history teacher with motivating his nationalist fanaticism. Years later, empowered as the Führer, he would radicalise German schools. They were tasked with focusing on 'racial awareness', in which science and biology were turned into indoctrination programmes promoting the Aryan race over the 'unworthy races' and fanning hated of the Jews to a lethal level. Further emphasis was placed on obsolete loyalty to the State as well as the dominance of the martial spirit, ensuring each child warrior was ready and committed to victory or death.

Appointed by Hitler to officiate as the Minister of Education was Bernhard Rust, whose credentials included the fact that he had been sacked from his own teaching position for sexual acts with a student. He was not charged with the crime as it was determined he was mentally unstable; however, Rust later qualified for his Nazi ministerial position, during which he ordered all Jewish teachers be dismissed from German schools and universities. By 1932 more than 30 per cent of teachers were sworn Nazi Party members. With the establishment of re-education camps for teachers, comprising a mandatory month-long immersion, two-thirds of grade school teachers had been processed by 1938.

Many teachers, often enthusiasticlly, fully allied themselves to Nazi doctrine, but those who did not found their authority undermined by Hitler Youth members who acted as spies, reporting 'disloyal' actions to their supervisors. There were teachers and students who resisted, however, but at their own peril. One such incident was reported by Herbert Lutz of Cologne, who recalled: 'My favorite teacher was my math teacher. I remember that one day he asked me a question. I was wearing my uniform, and I stood up, clicked my heels, and he blew up. The teacher shouted, "I don't want you to do this. I want you to act like a human being. I don't want machines. You're not a robot."'

Children were encouraged by promises of money as a reward if they reported on their parents, since according to Nazi doctrine: 'Your real father is the Führer, and being his children you will be the chosen ones, the heroes of the future.' Meanwhile, parents noticed that their children increasingly became 'strangers, contemptuous of traditions or religion, and perpetually barking and shouting like pint-sized Prussian sergeant-majors'.

As of January 1934, one year after Hitler's ascension to power, it was compulsory for schools to educate their pupils 'in the spirit of National Socialism'. Overall emphasis was placed on emotional rather than analytical responses. By the summer of that year, Rust, the Minister of Education, announced that Wednesday evenings and Saturdays would be devoted to Hitler Youth activities, while Saturday would now be known as *Staatsjugendtag*, the 'State's Day for Youth'.

As the teacher entered the classroom, children stood and gave the Hitler salute, with reverence for the Führer being instilled on a messianic level. Teachers often read from the virulent anti-Semitic outpourings of Nazi fanatic Julius Streicher, editor of the notorious and pornographic anti-Semitic publication *Der Sturmer*, who was also complicit in the production of Nazi codified textbooks echoing its sentiments.

Streicher, a known sadist and rapist, penned three children's books, with some 100,00 copies passing through the school system as part as the pervasive hate campaign focused on the Jews, and one forming the foundation for formulating and carrying out the Holocaust. The first of such books, illustrated with garish anti-Semitic illustrations, was titled *Trust No Fox on his Green Heath ... And no Jew on his Oath*. A sampling of the text reads:

> The Father of the Jews is the Devil,
> At the cration of the world
> The Lord God conceived the races:
> Red Indians, Negroes, and Chinese,
> And Jew-boys, too, the rotten crew.
> And we were also on the scene:
> We Germans midst this motley medley-
> He gave them all a piece of earth
> To work with the sweat of their brow.
> But the Jew-boy went on strike at once!
> For the Devil rode him from the first.
> Cheating, not working, was his aim;
> For lying, he got first prize
> In less than no time from the Father of Lies,
> Then he wrote it in the Talmud.

Thousands of young, malleable children took it as scripture.

Another area negatively affecting children's educational growth was the Hitler Youth movement's unending series of events, outings, camps, competitions, marches and rallies, which caused the wide-scale loss of student attendance, with physical activities outweighing intellectual training. Traditional studies of history no longer focused on the classics but on the history of the Nazi Party. As intended, indoctrination had supplanted education.

National Socialism bore a patriarchal approach to education, in that women were in effect excluded by policy. In January 1934, girls who had graduated from elementary school and were seeking admission to higher education at university found themselves facing a stringent quota, their number limited to one-tenth of the male students seeking entry, all toward shunting the girls toward domestic occupations. As Hitler was securing his power base in 1933, some 18,000 women were then currently attending university. By 1939, that number had been reduced to less than 5,500. Not only was female access to education limited, so were the number that were allowed to become teachers.

In turn, the Nazi Party developed the National Mother Service, one of its legions of bureaucracies – in this case one that attempted to encourage German women to focus on their new State-approved duties as mothers. One edict proclaimed: 'The purpose of the National Mother Service is political schooling. Political schooling for the woman is not a transmission of political knowledge, nor the learning of Party programmes. Rather, political schooling is shaping to a certain attitude, an attitude that out of inner necessity affirms the measures of the State, takes them into women's life, carries them out and causes them to grow and be further transmitted.' The task of discerning the meaning behind such statements no doubt further muddied the waters for young women seeking their place in the Third Reich. Party ideologue and Propaganda Minister Josef Goebbels chimed in with his own requirements for German women, announcing in 1934: 'Your duty is to produce at least four offspring in order to ensure the future of the national stock.'

In regards to German youth and the role of religion, Germany found itself traditionally divided geographically between strong Catholic and Protestant affiliations. Hitler, himself a lapsed Catholic, often proclaimed that Providence was on his side, relating to both his military successes and his escapes from assassination. He saw traditional religion as an impediment to the new faith offered by National Socialism. Toward that goal, traditional religious holidays were re-purposed with semi-pagan and Nazi symbolic trappings. Along those lines, the Nazi youth minister and Hitler Youth leader, Baldur von Schirach, commanded schoolchildren to recite a pre-meal prayer/poem of his own making. Though giving a nod to God, it now equated faith with the *Führer*.

> Führer, my Führer given me by God,
> Protect and preserve my life for long.
> You rescued Germany from its deepest need.
> I thank you for my daily bread.
> Stay for a long time with me, leave me not.
> Führer, my Führer, my faith, my light
> Hail my Führer.

Inner circle power wielder Martin Bormann summed up the Nazi Party's stance on religion on 6 June 1941 when he stated: 'National Socialist and Christian concepts cannot be reconciled. The Christian churches build on the ignorance of people and are anxious so far as possible to preserve this ignorance in as large a part of the populace as possible; only in this way can the Christian churches retain their power. In contrast, National Socialism rests on scientific foundations.' Later, on 10 December 1943, he added this caveat: 'Make sure that none of our children gets depraved and diseased by the poison of Christianity, in whatever dosage.'

Borman, Hitler's private secretary, considered by many as the second most powerful figure in Germany during the latter years of the Third Reich, remained loyal to Hitler to the end, taking control of Germany in the final days of the war. His death, or possible surival and escape to South America, remain a matter of controversy. On 28 August 1944, with the Russians steamrolling in from the east and the Allies advancing from the west after the Normany landings in June, Borman gave the following advice to German children: 'Never play with matches! Never touch explosive charges, anti-aircraft shells or duds! If others want to play with them, take to your heels at once! Never jump into the water when you're hot! Never swing on railings! Never go with strangers who priomise sweets or other things! Never fire a rifle or use a catapult where other people are about!'

Even music was served up by the State as an integral part of the indoctrination process. Hitler Youth leader Baldur von Schirach employed it to maximum effectiveness, including writing several songs himself, while the Nazi State published many song books, often dramatically illustrated. The lyrics were tailored to numerous marching, campfire and even Christmas songs. Group singing, rather than solo presentations, were emphasised, all toward group cohesion and 'solidarity with the State'.

Examples of the popular songs include 'Wir sind die Hitler-Jugend' (We are Hitler Youth); 'Sturmführer Wessel' (Storm Leader Wessel); 'Blonde und Braune Buben' (Blonde and Black Jackboots); 'Und wenn wir marschieren, Vorwärts!' (We March Forward!); and 'Wir sind das Heer vom Hakenkreuz' (We are the Army of the Swastika).

One example of the lyrics regarding the swastika and flag begins with a stanza that translates:

Look! Our flag flies oe'r our noble ranks!
With an iron clank from flank to flank!
We are marching for Hitler
For Freedom and Bread
With the flag of the Youth
That flies overhead!
Yes, our flag in triumph nobly flies!
Yes, our flag is reaching toward the sky!
To the ends of the Earth, and the last of our breath
Yes, the flag means more than death.

Prussian Salute
This photo of a young girl wearing an ornate turn-of-the-century helmet was glued to card and posted from Munich on 2 February 1915 during the second year of the First World War.

Full Regalia
In a pre-Third Reich group portrait, young children have donned the uniform of the *Reichswehr*, the Germany Army. Some wear paper hats, others the Prussian spiked helmet or *Pickelhaube* and one, standing in the center, wears a First World War era M-16 steel helmet, or *Stahlhhelm*, as well as a complete uniform. Many also carry toy rifles and swords. Not one child is smiling.

At Attention
The power and attraction of the military ethos runs deep in German culture, having been seeded centuries earlier by the Germanic tribes who often fought among themselves or against a common enemy such as the Romans, as a result creating heroes in German lore later trumpeted by Nazi propaganda.

Wir halten durch!

'We will Persevere!' – First World War Postcard
So states a colourised postcard dated 18 October 1915 as sent to a German infantryman at the battlefront. During this month several major battles raged during the First World War, including Gallipoli, Ypres and Loos. Poison gas (chlorine) was used for the first time on the battlefield by both sides. At this point the Germans seem to have the Allies on the run, but three years later the war is lost for Germany. As its allies vacate the war one after the other, Germany finds itself on its own. Its commander in the West, Ludendorff, tells his superior, von Hindenburg, that they must seek an Armistice; the two inform the Kaiser, who agrees. It comes as a shock for the government, the foot soldier and the German civilian, all having been kept uninformed by the German High Command as to the steady losses and poor condition of the troops.

Off to Fight for the Kaiser
A First World War-era postcard employs images of children to convery a patriotic message.

In the Image of the Father
During the 1800s and early 1900s the cult of
militarism was deply woven into the German
social fabric. As a result children's games
reflected on their military futures, traditionally
a means of advancement, both socially and
financially.

Rudolf and Mina Hess, Brother and Sister
The photograph of the future Deputy Führer
of Nazi Germany, taken sometime in the late
1890s to early 1900s, was published in May
1941 after being discovered in Bristol, Virginia,
by Mrs E. L. Upchurch, the widow of Hess's
brother, Gustave, had who lived in Bristol until
his death in April 1920. On 10 May 1941, Hess,
without notifying Hitler, suddenly flew from
Augsburg, Germany, to Scotland, where he
parachuted and was captured. His intentions are
still controversial; purportedly he was seeking
support from English royalty to join Germany in a
war against communist Russia. However, depsite
the fact he had no direct connections to Nazi war
crimes that transpired after his capture, he was
imprisoned in virtual solitary confinement for
more than forty-five years until his death in 1987
by apparent suicide. No other Nazi war criminal
was ever inprisoned for such a long span. As
Hitler, Himmler, Goring and Borman had escaped
justice by suicide, Hess was the only surviving
member of the Nazi hierachy, even though
Hitler himself had declared him insane and Hess
himself unable to provide a rational defence
during his trial.

The Children's Crusade, 1925
In another pre-Third Reich German photo, children, apparently armed, have joined members of
the *Freikorps*, various nationalistic groups of First World War veterans as well as the unemployed
and discontented who were at odds with the Weimar Republic and its democratic programmes.
The groups were a breeding ground for SA and Nazi Party members.

'One for All, All for One'
A photo postcard image dated 29 August sometime in the later 1920s records a youth group's
outing, one of their banners proclaiming the famous adage from Alexandre Dumas' novel
The Three Musketeers. By order of the Nazi State, all youth groups fell under its sway, save for
some religious groups that initially resisted.

Father and Daughters, 17 January 1937
The professional studio photograph juxtaposes an army officer in his *waffenrock* parade dress uniform with his two beautifully dressed daughters. Within two years all three will be caught up in a war that offers no mercy to man, woman or child. In this year Germany will send military aid, including the Condor Legion of the Luftwaffe, to aid the fascists under Franco engaged in the Spanish Civil War. It is also the year that Hitler's Germany spreads out the red carpet for Italy's Mussolini. The German economy was virtually booming and the Third Reich was ascending in international stature.

Christmas 1937
Two children, the boy wearing the uniform of the Heere (Army), stand rather uncomfortably for their photo as several NCOs, including a master sergeant (double cuff rings), appear in the background.

Pre-War Wedding Party, 1938
Several children join a large group portrait surrounding an NCO and his new wife. Of note are the conspicuous display of Christian crosses worn by two women, religion being barely tolerated by the Nazi State. Also visibile in the back row, far right, is a bow-tie-wearing man displaying a Nazi Party pin – Germany's new religion. 1938 was a high point for Nazi Germany after Hitler's successes with the assimilation of the Czech Sudetendland and Austria without a shot fired, further enbolding the Führer.

Detail of Wedding Party Photo
One wonders what fate awaits the the smiling faces. The two solidiers are already wearing Austrian and Czech service ribbons and the new war is only months away.

Floral Arrangements
In a pre-war wedding photo two children appear as flower girls as the bride smiles into the camera, her new husband in formal uniform apparently preferring to present a profile.

Wartime Wedding
Wearing both his combat ribbon and wound badge, a soldier has returned from the battlefront to celebrate a wedding.

Breeding for the New Order

Future Soldier
Wearing his father's overseas army cap, a small
boy clutches his sister's hand.

'My First School Gear'
A young boy proudly presents the chalk slate provided for his first day in school.

The Little Corporal
While the adults smile in the background, a young *Heer* (Army) recruit salutes the camera.

Silver Medal Mother and Hitler Youth as the Center of Attention
Gathered for a family portrait then fashioned into a photo postcard, the proud parents have
apparently produced eight children. The six sisters bookend the older son, while the youngest,
and the only one in uniform, has taken centre place, albeit on a chair closer to the ground. The
blonde- and dark-haired women have been posed as separate groups. Two more children and the
mother would qualify for the coveted Gold Medal for Motherhood

Tomorrow the World
The Hitler Youth boy, defensive body
language apparent, regards the camera with a
steely gaze.

Greeting Committee
Somewhere on the Baltic Sea coast,
a group of children pose with two
Imperial German Navy war flags,
first introduced in 1888.

Hitler Salute?
A closer look reveals he may be
indicating his age of three.

Toy Soldiers

The depiction of a child wielding a sword bridges the gap between childhood fantasy and the natural progression toward becoming a German soldier. The image includes a demonised caricature of England hung over a well, the message relating to the next conquest – the overwhelming of Great Britain. A focal point of pride was the awarding to Hitler Youth members of the ceremonial dagger, as if it were a miniature sword. The small blade empowered the youth as 'armed children', serving to further sever parental control and moulding them into the proto-warriors of Nazi Germany.

Helping Hand

An army corporal, wearinig his overseas cap and button hole ribbon, indicating his entry into the Sudetenland, steadies his young son for a studio portrait.

Bauz! da geht die Türe auf,
Und herein in schnellem Lauf
Springt der Schneider in die Stub'
Zu dem Daumen-Lutscher-Bub.
Weh! Jetzt geht es klipp und klapp
Mit der Scher' die Daumen ab,
Mit der großen scharfen Scher'!
Hei! da schreit der Konrad sehr.

Als die Mutter kommt nach Haus,
Sieht der Konrad traurig aus.
Ohne Daumen steht er dort,
Die sind alle beide fort.

Der Struwwelpeter, 'Shock-Headed Peter', 1930s German Children's Book
First published in 1845, this macabre children's book saw many reprintings. With its use of illustrations and narrative it is viewed as a precursor to comic books; however its cautionary tales focused on horrendous punishment for misbehaving children, including having their thumbs amputated for the crime of sucking them. The book enjoyed popularity in Europe, and even famous American writer Mark Twain presented his own English translation. The book is still popular today and spawned various stage and film adaptations.

Army Father and Navy Son – Pre-War
While the soldier wears epaulets indicating the
76th Infantry, the boy's cap carries the name of the
light cruiser *Emden*. First launched in 1925 by the
Reichsmarine, it served mainly as a training ship,
later as a mine layer and then in the Norwegian
invasion as the Second World War began. Manned
by a maximum crew of 683 and armed with obsolete
First World War guns, she also transported the
remains of Paul von Hindenburg to keep them from
falling into Soviet hands. While undergoing repairs in
Kiel she was badly damaged by British bombers, run
aground in the harbor and scuttled, then scrapped
in 1949. As for the father's attachment to the 76th
Infantry, first formed in August 1939 just prior to
the invasion of Poland, it was annihilated by the Red
Army at Stalingrad.

Zukinftiger Seemann, 'Future Sailor' –
Commercial Photo Postcard

One Step Closer...
Hitler Youth Naval Cadets could train aboard several *Kriegsmarine* training ships, including the *Horst Wessel* and the *Gorch Fock*.

Prototype
Wearing the downsized uniform of the *Kriegsmarine*, the German Navy, a young boy poses for a formal photo in church. A notation reads 'Paul – in commemoration of your communion, March 1937.' While Nazi dogma attempted to displace Christianity, more than 90 per cent of Germans remained members of their Catholic or Protestant churches, including 27 per cent off the SS.

Kriegsmarine Family – Pivotal Warship

Attired for a formal studio photo, along with a downsized rendition of the formal navy uniform, the young boy wears a cap stitched with the name *Atlantis*, which could indicate his father's ship. An auxillary cruiser designated *Schiff 16*, it was outfitted as a commerce raider preying on British merchant transport ships, sinking or capturing twenty-two and having traversed over 100,000 sea miles in 600 days. The *Atlantis* captured secret documents detailing the British military conclusion that it could not risk war with Japan. The information is thought to have encouraged the attack on Singapore and also against the American Navy at Pearl Harbor. However, *Atlantis* herself was later sunk by a British cruiser, the HMS *Devonshire*, on 22 November 1941.

Premature Sailor

Wearing a sailor's suit complete with Iron Cross, a boy's cap calls up the vaunted German dirigible: the *Graf Zeppelin*. However the cap and uniform refer to the German aircraft carrier of the same name, the only such naval vessel built for the Third Reich's *Kriegsmarine*. While the hull was launched on 8 December 1938, the project went unfinished and the ship was never operational. After the war it was used for bombing practice by the Soviets and sunk, the position of its wreckage off the coast of Poland not being verified until July 2006.

Herzlichen Glückwunsch zum Geburtstag

'Heartfelt Good Wishes on Your Birthday'
Postcard birthday greetings sent from the city of Kiel on 16 October 1938. During Nazi Germany's 1930s military expansion, the Kiel shipyards prospered with the construction of *Kriegsmarine* vessels, from battleships to submarines. In the previous month of September 1938, Jews were ruled secondary-class citizens and intermarriage was forbidden, while the swastika logo of the Nazi Party became the official national flag. The first U-boat flotilla was commissioned, with Kiel being the center of their production. Located at the southern end of the German Baltic coast, it provided an excellent natural harbor some 5 miles long. In the first half of August 1936 it was the scene of international sailing events, hosting part of the Berlin Olympics. Suffering some thirty-five bombing raids during the war, 80 per cent of the strategic city was destroyed.

Kriegsmarine Sailor and Daughter, July 1942
German forces on the Eastern Front continue
their successful onslaught of the Soviet Union,
occupying Sevastopol in the Crimea. In this
month the *Kriegsmarine* sees the temporary
decommissioning for repairs of the battlecruiser
Gneisenau. First launched in December 1936,
she, along with sister ship *Scharnhorst*, raided
British shipping on the Atlantic. The *Scharnhorst*
was sunk by British ships in 26 December 1943
with only thirty-six of the 1,968 crewmembers
surviving. The *Gneisenau* survived several
attacks. With a crew of 1,669, she took part in the
invasion of Norway. Damaged, she was repaired,
before being damaged again by British air attack
in 1941. Repaired again, she was then more
severely damaged with many casualties while in
the dry dock in February 1942. On 27 March
1945 she helped block the harbor at Gydnia
(German-occupied Poland). After the war, in 1951,
she was sold as scrap metal. One of her gun turrets
is on display in a Norwegian musuem.

**Child Sailor – Commercial Postcard Sent
on 29 June 1943**

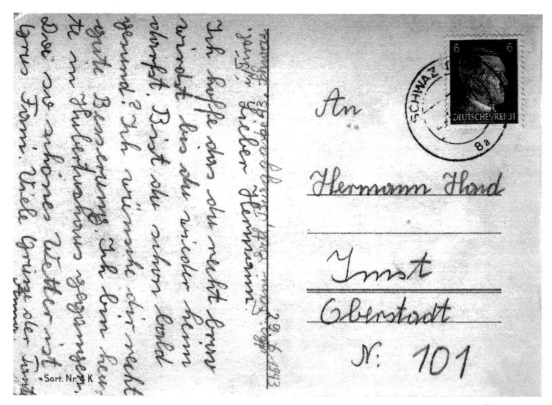

Postcard Message – Time to Write in the Bomb Shelter

The reverse of the card bore a handwritten message. Hermann Hond, perhaps a member of the *Kriegsmarine*, has received a postcard from his aunt who lives in Schwarza, Thuringia (central Germany), inquiring as to his health and the weather. It appears that he may be recovering from an illness or wound. His address is also in Thuriginia, specifically the municpality of Oberstadt.

Going by the postmark date of 29 June 1943, at this time German cities were under heavy RAF bombing, the U-boat war in the Atlantic had been lost with high casualties, and German forces were preparing for the fateful early July battle at Kursk, the largest tank battle in history, committing German and Soviet forces of 2 million men, 6,000 tanks and 4,000 aircraft. With both sides incurring heavy losses, it proved to be the last major German offensive effort on the Eastern Front.

'On to the Enemy!'
A future U-boat commander launches his
toy submarine off on patrol as illustrated by
Lungar Hauven, a famed German artist during
the 1940s and post-war. His artwork appeared
in many children's books and on a wide
variety of toys. In reality, U-boat personnel
suffered over 80 per cent losses, the highest
percentage of KIA for any branch of the
Third Reich military.

**'Young Flier' – Unposted Commercial
Postcard**
Flying a model airplane showing the swastika,
the small boy is depicted wearing pilot's cap and
goggles as well as pistol holster along with one
of the flowers he's picked from the ground at
his feet.

Future Luftwaffe Pilot and Hobby Horse
Notations on the reverse of this photo dated 1924 indicates that the child grew up to exchange his toy horse for a *Messerschmitt* or *Focke-Wulf*, and at some point during the war apparently flew out of the southern Italian town of Grottaglie, located on the Salento peninsula on the Adriatic coast. The photo's inscriptions contained no information regarding his ultimate fate.

On a Pedestal
A Luftwaffe NCO has equipped his son with his ceremonial dagger and one of his gloves.

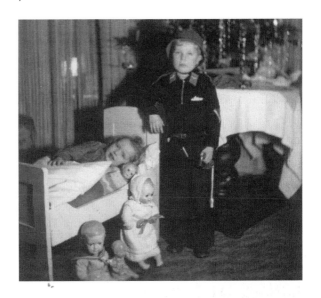

Role Playing

Dressed in his Luftwaffe corporal's uniform, possibly a just unwrapped Christmas gift, a young boy stands protectively over his sister, she herself enjoying her new dolls. Nazi theocracy was based on men as warrior and master, with women finding their life's role as housewife and producer of multiple children.

'Pimpf' on Guard

While *pimpf* is the German term for a prepubescent boy, it also refers to the youngest subset of the Hitler Youth structure – those aged six to ten.

'Edith und Ich'
Dwarfed by his older female companion as
well as an adult's Luftwaffe NCO's tunic,
a boy stands a bit apprehensively before
the camera. At some later point he wrote
the words on the reverse of the photo,
'Edith and I.'

Emulation – Luftwaffe Ground Troops

Feathery Fountain
Standing before a sculpture of acquatic birds, an SS man listens attentively to the young girl, perhaps his sister, holding his hand. His cap (*kepi*) appears to be decorated with what may be a mountain troop edelweiss insignia.

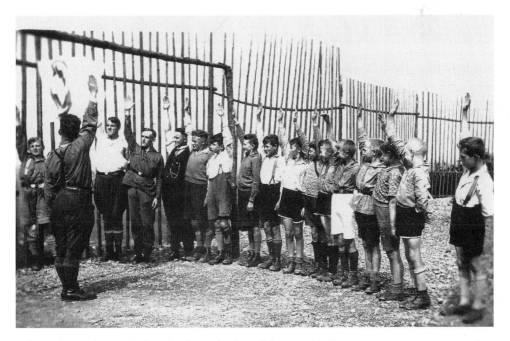

Mix and Match Pre-Hitler Youth Gathering, 6 August 1932
An assortment of ages and clothing styles appear among a gathering of Nazi Party supporters. All appear to be giving the Hitler salute, if a bit too vertical, or they may be volunteering for something. A rudimentary wooden enclosure seems to mark their camp grounds. This may be an SA-orchestrated gathering, as indicated by two of the men's uniforms. Although the SA had been banned in June of that year, in the following July the Nazi Party had gained 230 representaive members in the Reichstag. Hitler himself received nearly 14 million votes from the German public; however in the following November elections, Hitler's party would lose fifty-four Reichstag seats and 2 million votes, with the communists making major gains. Nevertheless, Hitler's cult of admiration had grown even stronger among German youth.

'The Volunteers' – Anti-Nazi Art

At first glance one might not realise this postcard bears a satirical illustration, much less one that sent Hitler into a seething rage. One of the most powerful, yet least known, examples of anti-war protests during the Third Reich was launched by a young nun named Sister Maria Innocentia. The world today for the most part knows her by another name and makes no connection between the Third Reich and her highly valued and universally loved figurines of angels and children. Her name was Berta Hummel, her signature appearing as 'H. I. Hummel'. While reproductions of Hummel figurines are numberless, her originals are today greatly valued by museums, but moreover her original paintings and drawings.

Seen here is a watercolour painting she titled *The Volunteers*. Two three-year-old boys goose-stepping from left to right are dressed in SA-style clothing. As one beats a drum, the other wears an unhappy expression and carries his rifle barrel incorrectly with the trigger side up. The old German script translates to 'Dear Fatherland, let there be peace!'

The official Nazi press railed against the painting when it first appeared, saying: 'There is no place in the ranks of German artists for the likes of her' and 'No, the beloved Fatherland cannot remain calm when Germany's youth are portrayed as brainless sissies', as her characters were said to be drawn to look like 'hydrocephalic, club-footed goblins'. The State also struck back by cutting the publisher's paper allotment and banning the sale in Germany of Hummel's drawings (including this postcard), as well as her popular porcelains. However they allowed foreign export to gain the much-needed foreign exchange currency to aid Nazi expansion.

A talented and well-trained artist, but also a very religious Catholic, Hummel became a Dominican nun within the order of St Francis of Assisi. For fifteen years she served the community and also taught art to local children. A contract to aid the convent resulted in the reproduction of her images into porcelain figures, which quickly fostered worldwide sales. Those revenues still benefit the convent's work.

Berta Hummel died from tuberculosis at thirty-seven in 1946, a year after the war ended.

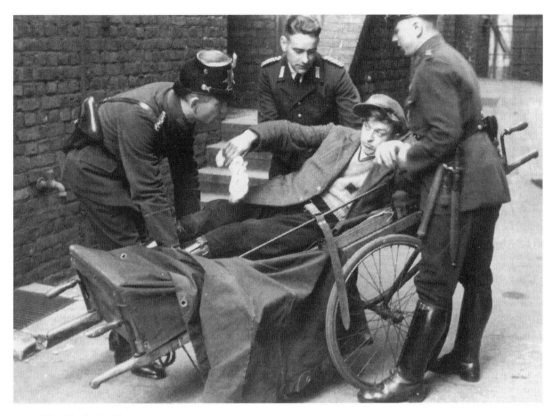

The Undesirables

Civilian policemen are photographed purportedly seeing to the needs of a handicapped boy as they unload him from his special cart. Eventually Nazi State-sponsored programmes to eliminate the mentally and physically disabled would result in the murder of over 200,000 people, with elements of the police taking part in their round-up and transport to the euthanasia centers.

Six centers for the extermination of mental asylum patients were established by January 1941 as part of the 'T-4' operation designed to purge German blood of the feeble-minded and genetically afflicted of all ages. The 'passports to death' were signed by the country's leading psychiatrists and pediatricians. Thousands would die by injection, starvation or in the facilities' relatively small gas chambers, taking twenty or less victims at a time, but serving as a rehearsal of techniques later employed on a mass scale in the death camps.

In 1941, Goebbels's film productions released *Ich Klage an* ('I Accuse'), whose storyline concerns a woman with an incurable disease who calls for her own 'termination' in order to save the State the expense of her medical care – an overt propaganda ploy to promote the Nazi State's euthanasia programme.

Traveler's Aid – Refused

A group of children gather in front of a Shell travel map as two soldiers contemplate their touring plans.

Nazi Germany attempted to gain control of the Royal Dutch Shell Group via the ruthless oil baron Sir Henri Deterding, a staunch anti-communist and early admirer of Hitler who initially offered Germany a year's worth of oil credit in 1935 as a war reserve but who refused the Nazi financial proposals. He died six months before the attack on Poland and the beginning of the war, which would eventually see the blitzkrieg grounded for lack of fuel.

Birth Rate in High Gear
A family of six poses proudly by their Opel automobile somewhere in the Baden (Heidelberg, Mannheim, Freiburg, Lake Constance) area of Germany, as indicited by the licence plate.

Four-Legged Friend
As a cow munches hay, a soldier's daughter perches on her father's shoulder for a photo.

Street Scene, June 1938

Parents and children stroll across the cobblestones on a sunny summer day, signs of prosperity apparent. Some five years into the Third Reich Germany's economy has recovered, the country buoyant with the bloodless annexation of Austria in March of that year. Anti-Jewish decrees mount and the famous Munich Temple is destroyed by Nazi thugs. The two boys wearing lederhosen will very likely soon trade them in for uniforms of Hitler Youth, and their sister the BdM, the girls' youth organisation.

Young Girl on a Tuffet, 1940

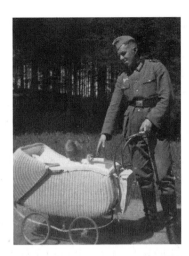

Popular Pram

An army private wearing an overseas service cap reaches for the hand of his child ensconced within a wicker baby carriage, a type often seen in photos of the era.

Pram Officer in a Doomed City

Notations on the reverse of the photo date it as having been taken on 9 August 1943 and processed at Photo-Gorner in the city of Dresden. Some two years hence, on the evening of 13 February 1945, near the ending of the war, Dresden and its civilian population was swallowed by cyclones of fire after waves of Allied bombers first dropped incendiary bombs, then high explosives designed to ignite them into a catastrophic firestone. Killed were an estimated 35,000 to 135,000 city residents as well as streams of refugees that had made their way to what they thought was a sanctuary city only to be literally evaporated into ash or suffocated in the city's crowded bomb shelters. Controversy still rages over the strategic importance of targeting 'The Florence of the Elbe', a city known as center for arts with few air defences. Allied planners point to its railway yards as important conductors of war materials, while others consider it a war crime.

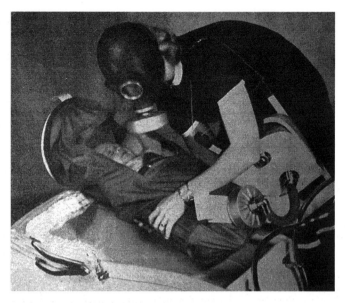

Baby Carriage Model
With memories of the horrors of poison gas attacks during the First World War as employed by both Germany and the Allies, advanced designs of gas masks suitable for all ages were developed.

Casting a Shadow
As their baby fidgets, blurring the image, a policeman and his wife attempt to pose for their studio portrait, their shadows cast against the backdrop.

Mobile police execution units were responsible for the murder of more than 1 million Jewish civilians in Eastern Europe during the 'Holocaust by bullets'. Over 150,000 children were shot, bayonetted, clubbed or buried alive. Many of the killers had children of their own. Post-war, very few were ever brought to justice.

Luftwaffe *Helferin*
A female auxillary member of the German Air
Force cradles her baby for a studio portrait.
Notations on the reverse read: 'Bonn 1942 … in
memory of your friend Leni.' Bonn, located on
the Rhine River in North Rhine Westphalia, was
reached by American forces on 7 March 1945
after the capture of Remagen Bridge enabled the
Allies to penetrate Germany. It would become
the provisional capital of West Germany after the
war's end.

Harvest Festival
Beautifully dressed children pose with their
mother and father, a highly decorated Luftwaffe
NCO (*stabsfeldwebel*), his uniform bearing the
Iron Cross (First and Second Class) as well as his
Air Crew Badge and Operational Flying Clasp.

Austrian Family – Assimilated Germans

Father, mother and ten children pose in traditional clothing, except for two sons, who are wearing the uniform of the German Army.

As of 8 March 1938, Austria was assimilated into Greater Germany, its draftable-aged citizens liable for conscription eventually finding over 1 million fighting for the Third Reich. Hitler, himself an Austrian, had been a corporal in the *Reichswehr* during the First World War. After the war was lost, the Allies regarded Austria as both victim and victimiser, while the Austrians themselves kept a low profile on the pro-Nazi activities.

May Day Parade

Several children have prepared for the annual celebration and carry traditional Bavarian flower poles while two boys serve as the wagon's 'horsepower'. Three of the boys wear traditional lederhosen. One of the swastika banners carries the name of a local newspaper while the other relates to the SA. As the image, processed by a Hans Hofer at his photography shop, possibly in Munich, appears to have been taken in the early 1930s, the boys were eventually of age to join the military during the war.

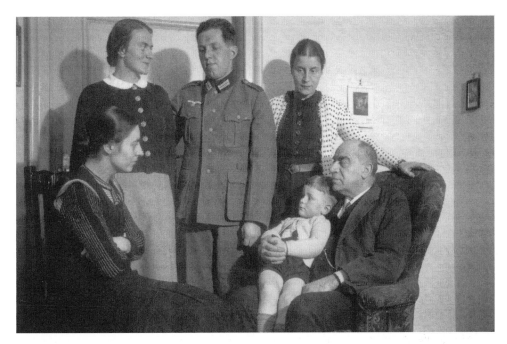

Centers of Attention

A newly minted army private joins with his seemingly related womenfolk while a grandfather holds his grandson. The seated woman, with somewhat defensively folded arms, appears to gaze at the child and man. Who, if anyone, will survive the war is unknown.

Mit Großmutter

Three generations find two in uniform, one a corporal in the army (far right) and one a policeman (center rear), joined by three children gathered around their *Oma* in a pre-war portrait.

Wounded Corporal and Family
A bespecticaled army corporal, his Wound Badge just visible, poses with wife and two sons, the youngest clutching a toy animal.

Sunday Best at Nenndorg
A family sits for their studio portrait, taken at Foto Remers, the photography studio located in the town of Bad Nenndorf. While his parents appear to be taking the photo session with a degree of seriousness, their son's expressions seems to convey the attitude of all children forced into such circumstances

Nenndorf's history began in the ninth century, and would later gain fame for its healing sulfur spring spas purportedly bringing relief for rheumatism, gout and skin diseases. Nazi-era planners saw to revamping the spa's facilities. Post-war the British operated a secret detention and interrogation center in the spa's structures, where 372 male and forty-four female high Nazi officials, diplomats and military officers were held, along with, strangely enough, communists. Complaints about the center's conditions prompted its closure in 1947. By the early 2000s Bad Nenndorf had become a rallying point for neo-Nazis, who congregated there to demonstrate against the so-called 'victims of the Allied torture camp'.

Bright Future

A *Kriegsmarine* officer and his stylishly dressed wife and son enjoy a family snapshot sometime in October 1941. In that month, Hitler triumphantly announced to the German population in Berlin the results of his war against the Bolsheviks and Slavic 'subhumans' in the Soviet Union: namely, the capture of 500,000 Russian POWs along with 22,000 guns, as well as the destruction of 18,000 tanks and 23,000 aircraft. Victory seems near at hand and the future seems bright for the children of the Third Reich.

Field Kitchen in Action

Notations on the reverse of the photo indicate that a Dr Wehmeyer is seen among the soldiers, identified as the staff physician as well as company chief. The officers in the foreground wear spurs on their boots, indicating their cavalry affiliations. The boys in the foreground are unidentified.

Home from the War
The photographer's shadow casts across a decorated soldier holding his son as the family dog stands close by.

'*Meiner Lieben*'
No doubt deliberatly positioned in the composition, the Supreme Leader watches over a decorated army NCO and son. The photo, dated 23 November 1943, finds Nazi Germany on the defensive in the east, yet fanatical allegience continues.

'In Memory of January 1944 with Ursula Born 3 September 1941' – A Coincidence of Events

When this family portrait was taken in the Silesian city of Lausitz, the Third Reich was on the defensive on the Eastern Front, Red Army forces pushing them back out of the Soviet Union. The 900-day siege of Lenningrad had been lifted, a million civilians having died from starvation, disease and bombings. Thousands of bodies became visible later during the spring thaw.

On 5 January 1944 the Russian journalist Vasily Grossman returned to his hometown of Berdichev in the Ukraine hours after its liberation from German occupation by the Red Army. There he learned of the fate of 30,000 of the city's Jewish inhabitants, including his mother – the victims of mass shootings. In a carefully orchestarted formula, the Germans first ordered the assembly of 1,500 young Jewish men and boys from the local ghetto, allegedly for agricultural labour. They were marched outside of town and shot. Their families in the ghetto never learned of their fate and the Germans had eliminated the individuals who could have potentially mounted a resistance. Grossman also learned that while some local Ukrainians aided in the murders, others saved some of their Jewish neighbours. He was also told by witnesses of German soldiers' sense of humour. In one instance they rounded up a number of old Jewish men and forced them to don their prayer shawls and enter the local synagogue to 'pray to God to forgive their sins against Germans'. Afterwards they locked the doors, set it afire and burned the Jews alive. It was a microcosm of uncountable such mass immolations that took place across Eastern Europe.

Also in January 1944, on the 21st, the Allies successfully land at Anzio, south of Rome, Axis ally Italy was soon out of the war, and six months later, in June, the Allies breached 'Fortress Europe' with 1.5 million troops.

Bavarian Fashion
An army officer wearing a uniform ribbon indicating service in the Czech actions appears with his young son in more traditional attire.

Balancing Act
A father and daughter perform for the camera.

Lunging Toward Soldierhood
A young boy happily plays at being a soldier, but as the
Thousand-Year Reich will last only twelve years he will be too
young to wear a full-sized uniform. Nevertheless, he may still
have had time to join the Hitler Youth and experience the terror
of the air war over Germany.

Special Toy from Gablonz, Christmas 1943
A young German boy and girl are photographed with what was very likely a new Christmas gift.
The wagon bears the words '*Corazza Spedition Gablonz*', which translates to 'Corazza Freight
Transport of Gablonz'.

Gablonz is a city in northern Bohemia/Czechoslovakia, known for centuries as a center for
glassware manufacture and famous for its beautiful and intricate Christmas tree decorations.
In March 1938, Britain and France, seeking to avoid war, acquiesced to Hitler's demands
for the return to Germany of the area known as the Sudetenland with its large population of
German-speaking residents. Seven years later, and in the wake of the defeat of Nazi Germany
and the arrival of Soviet forces, the Sudetenland *Volksdeutsche* were forcibly expelled by the
Czechs during the summer of 1945, including those living in Gablonz.

Approved Toys in a Damaged Photo
Wearing his toy helmet, a boy commands a Luftwaffe battery of 88 mm anti-aircraft cannon and support elements including an electrified searchlight.

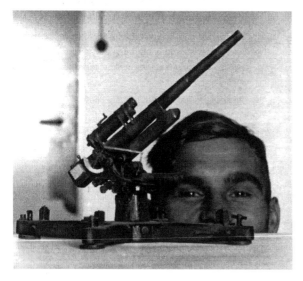

Iconic Cannon
A young boy appears behind a model of the 88 Flak gun, a multi-purpose anti-aircraft, anti-tank, anti-fortifications, anti-personnel weapon capable of firing various explosive projectiles, including a 21 lb shell some 7 miles. The boy, and hundreds more like him, would man the guns in the last months of the war in a vain attempt to ward off the non-stop Allied air raids targeting Germany's cities.

Das Maſchinengewehrneſt

Am Wegrain unter den alten Weidenbäumen hat man ein gutes Schußfeld nach vorn, nach rechts und nach links. Das ist also der richtige Platz, um ein schweres Maschinengewehr einzubauen. Gegen Sicht von der Erde und aus der Luft sind Waffe und Schützen durch das Laub der Bäume und durch das hohe Gras getarnt. Nun mag der Feind kommen. Der Gewehrführer ist auf alles vorbereitet: Die Entfernungen zu den wichtigsten Geländepunkten sind ermittelt, und Munition ist bereitgelegt. Ein Pfiff oder Wink des Hauptmanns, und das Maschinengewehr prasselt los: fünfhundert Schuß und mehr in der Minute. Da bricht jeder feindliche Ansturm blutig zusammen. Die schweren Maschinengewehre bilden somit das Gerippe der infanteristischen Verteidigung. Erst wenn sie durch die Kampfwagen, die Artillerie und Minenwerfer außer Gefecht gesetzt sind, kann die Infanterie des Angreifers auf Erfolg rechnen. Aber auch der Angreifer wird ohne schwere Maschinengewehre nicht auskommen. Er braucht ihr Feuer, um den Verteidiger in Deckung zu zwingen und zwischen ihn und seine heraneilenden Verstärkungen einen Feuerriegel zu legen. Jedes Bataillon des deutschen Heeres hat außer seinen drei Schützen-Kompanien noch eine Maschinengewehr-Kompanie. Auf dem Marsche haben es ihre Mannschaften besser als die Kameraden von den Schützen-Kompanien. Sie können zeitweise auf den pferdebespannten Wagen aufsitzen. Dafür haben sie auf dem Gefechtsfelde an dem schweren Gerät um so ärger zu schleppen. Als Maschinengewehrschütze werden daher besonders kräftige Wehrpflichtige ausgesucht, während sonst für die Infanterie vorzugsweise Wehrpflichtige mit geraden und kräftigen Beinen in Frage kommen.

Das Maschinengewehrnest – Children's Book Illustrated
One of several color images, in this case of a machine gun nest, appearing in a book describing the German Army and its weapons as printed for young readers.

Elastolin MG08 Gun Carrier, *c.* 1930
Elastolin was a trademark registered by O&M Hausser (*O&M Haußer*) for the toy soldiers and other types of figures it manufactured using wire armature frames overlaid with a composite of sawdust, glue and clay (*kaolin*). They were then hand painted.

On the Knee of the SS
In a photo dated 22 June 1940, three children join three SS men and their machine gun in the French city of Orgeville, German forces having occupied France in the previous May after a six-week campaign.

Portable Weapon of Mass Destruction
A 1930–40s vintage German children's toy soldier operates a flamethrower. The composite toy figure bears the imprint of the Gloria company on the underside of its base.

'Flamethrowers Attack!
The cover image of the 98th issue of *War Booklets for German Youth* illustrates the use of a *flammenwerfer* against French soldiers. From 1940 through December 1942, a total of 156 were published on a weekly basis, all including a call to join the military. An additional fourteen special editions were allocated just for Hitler Youth members.

**'Gas Masked Grenade Thrower'–
Hauser-Elastolin, 1920s**
Pre-war and Third Reich German children
alike played with these popular toys, which
came modeled after army, navy and air force
personnel brandishing a variety of weapons.
The company was founded in 1904 by brothers
Otto and Max Hausser and relocated during
the Nazi era to Neustadt bei Coburg, the heart
of the German toy and doll region where they
focused on German military and Nazi figures.
This figure was unearthed in a bombed-out area
of Nuremberg.

**General in Miniature Who Would Lose
his Position**
This Elastolin image is a rendering of General
Werner von Blomberg, a First World War
hero and the Third Reich's first General Field
Marshal of the Wehrmacht. Blomberg was
appointed Minister of Defence in 1935 but
was eventually dismissed in 1938 through the
machinations of Goering and Himmler, as
well as Hitler, who wanted him out of the way,
subsequently appointing himself Commander of
the Wehrmacht.

SS Men Present Arms

The lead toy soldiers featured articulated arms that could raise their rifles.

The double-lightning-bolt symbol associated with the SS insignia had a rather prosaic derivation. Known as the SS Sig Runes, the design was accidentally designed in 1931 by Walter Heck, then an SA company commander. He happened to notice the similarity between the two sig runes and the SS (*Shutzstaffel*) initials. He offered the design to the SS, who paid him a mere 2.5 Reichsmarks for the symbol that was to become one of the most feared and hated in European history. The black dress uniforms of Nazi Germany were designed and produced by prominent fashion designer Hugo Boss, while slave labour in concentration camps produced most of the regular military uniforms.

Sibling Solidarity

Three brothers gather for a pensive pre-war portrait. One wears the uniform of the *Riechsarbeitsdienst* (RAD), the mandatory German labor service, a prelude to military service.

Military Miniature
The diminutive soldier wears cavalry jodphurs while his regular army-uniformed companion gives the Hitler salute.

Non-uniformity
Older brothers join hands with their unusually dressed sister.

Official Identification Photo
The triangular patch (*Gebietsdreick*)
identifies the Nord Nordmark
geographical region and membership
for this member of the DJV (*Deutsches
Jungvolk*). Nordmark is a section of
northern Germany containing the city of
Brandenburg and bordered by the Oder
and Elbe rivers.

Portrait of a DJV
The DJV (*Deutsches Jungvolk*) was
the category of Hitler Youth for ten to
fourteen year olds. If he successfully
passed various tests, including a
knowledge of Nazi dogma, all the verses
to the 'Horst Wessel Song' (NSDAP
official song), a hike for a day and a
half, the ability to lay telephone wires
and fire small caliber weapons, this DJV
member could matriculate into the Hitler
Youth proper.

Tabula Rosa
The official song of the Hitler Youth was titled '*Es zittern die morschen Knochen*' or 'The Rotten Bones are Trembling', referring to the effects of the First World War. The 1932 version included the words 'Germany is ours and tomorrow, the whole world,' but in 1937 it was modified for Hitler Youth use with revised lyrics 'For today, Germany hears us.'

'*Deutschen Waffen*' (German Weapon)
A young boy examining a bayonet is the subject of a bronze sculpture by Third Reich 'approved' aritst Hias Lauterbacher, as displayed in the Munich House of German Art museum and reprinted as a commerical postcard. Placing the power of the blade in the hands of German youth was accomplished both symbolically via art and in reality with the awarding of the Hitler Youth dagger, a scaled-down version of the army bayonet that bore the inscription 'Blood and Honor'.

Baldur von Schirach – Hitler's Pied Piper Who Sought Atonement
Von Schirach's image appears on a collectible card found in cigarette packs in a series spotlighting leading personalities of the Third Reich.

Appointed in October 1931 as chief of youth activities for the Nazi Party, the charismatic von Schirach, barely twenty-six, was actually three-quarters American – his father a US citizen until he joined the Prussian Army and two of his ancestors signees of the Declaration of Independence. Advocating the 'Youth Leads Youth' dictum, von Schirach was blindly devoted to National Socialism and an anti-Semite as well as anti-Christian. However, he would keep the post until August 1940 when he was demoted to Governor of Vienna after expressing concerns about the treatment of Jews. Convicted of complicity in war crimes and admitting he poisoned the minds of German youth due to his own obsession with Hitler, he served twenty years in prison and became a strong advocate against Nazism, taking public responsibility for not doing more to prevent the death camps. Released in 1966, he lived quietly until dying in his sleep in 1974.

Role Models
Two young soldiers, with the *gefreiter* or corporal on the right apparently in the cavalry, as indicated by his lined trousers, bookend perhaps a Hitler Youth family member.

'Clarinet Solo'
The text on the reverse of this collectible card found in packages of cigarettes depicts a musician entertaining children with his clarinet. The caption on the reverse reads: 'During military maneuvers, music is the special joy of young and old. Our artists rarely have a more greatful audience for our images.'

Talented Family
Mother at the accordion, father with mandolin and son with flute and wearing a child's army uniform, perhaps a Christmas gift, gather round the celebration table. On the wall behind them hangs the Führer's portrait.

A Different Drummer
A Hitler Youth *pimpf* or cub wears the 'swallow's nest' shoulder insignia, identifying him as a musician. The insignia was also worn by adults serving as musicians in the German military.

A Hitler Youth *Pimpf* magazine article published in August 1944 as Germany reeled after one defeat after another titled 'The Faith of the Youth is the Foundation of Victory' opened with: '20 July 1944 is the tenth anniversary of the existence of the SS as an independent organisation of the NSDAP. Our SS divisions stand in unshakable, heroic struggle on all fronts. SS men face the enemy as they have always faced the enemy. Believing in Germany and the Führer, they will master fate. The SS remains what it always was: The Führer's dependable, sacrificial fighting troop.'

Formal Attire
Dressed in top hat and tails with an umbrella
draped over his arm, a man poses with a young
boy wearing a First World War-style *stahlhelm*
with a bayonet at his side and a cigar clenched
in his mouth. The photo was turned into a
mailable postcard.

Not Yet in Uniform
Having just attended what appears to be a
church Communion event, a Luftwaffe motor
transport NCO (*Shirrmeister*) joins his son in
his Sunday best. The photo has been printed in
postcard format.

Aryan German Family
Dressed for the occasion, a family poses for the camera. Their Hitler Youth son is the center of attention, although he stands closer to his father, who wears a Nazi Party pin. The mother wears a summer floral frock and fashionable shoes plus gauntlet-type gloves while the father carries a cane, possibly a result of First World War service. The boy has hooked his hand over his belt, a pose very reminscent of one often assumed by Hitler during public appearances and official photos.

Alternate Aryan Family with Father in Uniform

'June 1942 in Gowlitz'

Notations on the reverse of the photo indicate the location was Gowlitz (Gorltiz), Germany's easternmost city. It was also the location for Goebbel's infamous 'Total War' speech, given on 18 February 1943. Prior to the outbreak of war Gowlitz was the site of a Hitler Youth training camp, before being transformed into a POW camp housing Polish, Russian, British Commonwealth, Belgian, French and some 1,800 American prisoners. During the closing days of the war, and as the liberating Red Army advanced, the British and Americans POWs were forced on a 'death march' deeper into Germany.

School Photo Day

Children and instructors gather for a group portrait taken on the steps of one of the Hitler Youth schools set up across Germany. Intellectual pursuits and analytical thinking were proscribed in favor of phyical fitness training and ideological indoctrination. With Germany's pre-Third Reich educational standards severely eroded, an entire generation thereby suffered from a stunted education, albeit well-moulded into citizens of the Third Reich, where the individual was subjugated to the State.

Hitler Youth and BdM School Portrait
The single-lightning-bolt insignia of the Hitler Youth (one half of the SS insignia) glints in the sun.

Deviating from the Norm
As one boy gives the Hitler salute with one hand, the other holding a bottle of milk, another crouches low, as if trying to the avoid the camera.

The Crown of Steel
On the annual armed forces celebration, German boys have been allowed into a Wehrmacht vehicle, where they have donned helmets, much to their enjoyment. The cigarette-smoking soldiers have added flowers to the barrels of their Mauser rifles, at least for the day.

Collecting for Winter Relief
On the streets of Berlin, a bouquet-equipped Hitler Youth boy receives a donation from a fox stole-wearing woman. The image appeared on a collectible cigarette card, initially a popular pastime until Nazi social planners cracked down on smoking as an unhealthy habit.

Commercial Postcard celebrating Annual Armed Forces Day, 1942
Children, including a Hitler Youth member in coveralls and carrying a Winter Relief Collection
(KWH) container, are depicted enjoying a ride with a *Kradschutze* aboard his motorcycle sidecar
during celebrations in the 17th military district located in the Vienna, Lower and Oberdonau region.

***Winterhilfe* Tin Trinket**
An image of a priest comforting two children
is the theme of this donation gift, inscribed
with the words 'Vincent helps the abandoned',
which is a reference to St Vincent, an
eighteenth-century French Catholic priest
who served the poor. The 'St' reference did
not appear on the inscription due to the Nazi
anti-religion stance.

Lightning Strikes Once...
A squad leader carries the single-lightning-bolt insignia for the Hitler Youth movement. Seen
as potential members of the SS, a second lightning bolt may strike in their future. Their black
outfits, usually worn in winter, also mimicked the uniforms of the elite Panzer units.

The Führer Speaks

A lone Hitler Youth boy, the single lightning bolt affixed below his regional emblem, is surrounded by womenfolk as the group apparently listens to a radio broadcast. The Third Reich kept up a steady barrage of music of one kind or the other, from the constant thump of marching boots and brassy military bands, to street orchestra recitals to radio broadcasts of German classical to light romantic fare, all part of the 'emotion over intellect' campaign that party ideology promoted. The constant soundtrack also engulfed citizens and soldiers in a litany of songs designed to promote morale, military aggressiveness and Nazi political and racist propaganda. Everyone sang, from school children to the SS.

Warning Label

'Keep in mind that monitoring foreign transmitters is a crime against the national security of our people. By order of the Führer it can result in severe prison terms.'

A note affixed to a German civilian radio reminds 'eavesdroppers' of the potential penalties that were often applied to offenders, many turned in by their neighbors and, in some cases, parents by their Hitler Youth and BdM children. In one example a woman, after hearing a British broadcast that stated her neighbor's son, reported killed in action, was actually alive and well as a POW, gave the good news to her neighbour, only to have her report her to the Gestapo.

On Her Father's Shoulders
A young soldier in a rumpled and worn uniform, possibly home on leave, pauses for a family photo.

Brothers and Twins Sisters, 1940
The older brother wears his overseas cap, announcing he has been to France (invaded in May), while his brother wears his dark Hitler Youth winter uniform.

Ceremonial Bystanders

A group of Hitler Youth in their black winter uniforms stand as a group as their elders participate in some of the relentless events to promote Nazi Party military and political agendas. In the foreground stand two officers of the horse-mounted cavalry, while behind them stand a mix of party members, army, navy and SA men in this pre-war photo.

Farewell Photo

A boy carries his bedroll while on his way to a Hitler Youth camp. Perhaps his mother or father took this farewell snapshot before losing him to the party's control. His *Gebietsdreick* shoulder patch indicates he belongs to the East Sachenhausen section.

Fun and Games

Well-armed Makebelieve Indians
As portrayed in American films of the
period, cowboys and Indians were
very popular in Germany despite Nazi
propaganda portraying the US as a land of
violent gangsters and bloodthirsty savages.
The boys have gathered up a bow and
arrow, tomahawk and tomtom, and even a
few feathers for a headdress. The October
1938 issue of *Der Pimpf* magazine focused
on the American Sioux, with the story
conceding that, while a strong race, they
were unable to withstand the even stronger
white race.

Ubiquitous Accordion

One of the most popular musical instruments in Germany, and thus traveling both with Hitler Youth at home and soldiers in the battlefield, was the accordion. The instrument initially met with resistance from the Nazi social planners, who viewed the instrument as too crude to join the Third Reich culture and tried to ban it, but after Hohner and others, in answer to this threat of exclusion, began producing large quantities of classical music for the highly portable instrument, the State relented and authorised its use.

Campsite

Groups of Hitler Youth boys gather outside their tents, which have been pitched along the seaside sand dunes.

Hitler Youth Jamboree and Mascot – Altenberg
The town of Altenberg is located in the Saxony area of central Germany, some 32 km from Dresden and very near the Czech border.

The numerous Hitler Youth programmes promoted a culture of dominance reinforced in a paramilitary fashion to both prepare the young for leadership and to instill blind obedience. Physically exhausting and mind-numbing techniques were developed to depersonalise their responses and encourage group adhesion, further encouraging the use of unhesitant and pitiless violence against the perceived enemy.

At the Microphone
Much to the amusement of his audience, a Hitler Youth boy appears to be singing a song. The repetition of party slogans and ideology via group songfest was a constant and effective means of indoctrination.

1938 was a banner year for Hitler after his successes in the Sudetenland and the *Anschluss* of Austria. It also saw the number of full-time Hitler Youth leaders rise to 8,000, further expanding via 720,000 part-time leaders. If parents refused to allow their children to join the programme, they were often taken from their parents by the State.

Early Hitler Youth Encampment at Korinburg, Austria, 29 April 1935
The style of caps as well as the design of the armband *hackenkreuz* (swastika) are telltale signs
of the early days of the Hitler Youth movement. Leaning against the tent are a trio of grim-faced
boys clad in steel-tipped hobnail boots, apparently sharing a snack.

Marked
A young Hitler Youth member from the city of
Glogau carries a serious wound on his face. Injuries
during training exercises were common as the boys
were encouraged to maximum competition. He wears
the later design single-lightning-bolt belt buckle,
inscribed with the words *Blut und Ehre* – 'Blood and
Honor'. Later he might wear the SS buckle inscribed
with its motto 'My honor is loyalty'.

Glogau, in lower Silesia, became a Nazi stronghold
of resistance in the last days of the war before its
capture by Red Army forces. Turned over to Poland
post-war, it was renamed Glogow, its German
population being violently expelled.

Proud Hitler Youth Member of Amberg
This photo was processed at *Foto-Atelier Amberger* in the south-eastern Bavarian city of Amberg, itself a microcosm for endemic German anti-Semitism later inflamed by Nazi doctrine. In 1298, thirteen members of its small Jewish community were murdered during a series of massacres. Then, in 1403, its now larger community was forcibly expelled, and its synagogue converted into a church. By 1942, with the Nazi State at its zenith, only twelve Jews were still found living in Amberg.

Leipzig Hitler Youth
Minus their knee socks, two boys have donned their uniforms for a parental photo that was then turned into a postcard for mailing.

Leipzig, some 100 miles south-west of Berlin, was the home of composer Felix Mendelssohn. The Jewish composer's statue was destroyed by the pro-Nazi deputy mayor in 1937, causing the anti-Nazi mayor to resign. On Kristalnacht, in November 1938, the city's famous synagogue was destroyed. Leipzig was also home to one of the *Lebensborn* programme centres that sought to produce children between SS officers and unmarried women housed for that purpose. End of war combat saw fierce block-by-block fighting between Nazi defenders, including Hitler Youth, against American troops. It also saw female members of 'Organisation Werewolf' (formed by Goebbels to harass Allied forces) pouring boiling water onto the heads of Allied soldiers passing beneath their windows.

'Who is This?'
On the reverse of this photo portrait of a Hitler
Youth member someone has written '*Wer is
Das?*' – 'Who is this?' The patch on his arm
above the swastika identifies him as a member
of the Nord Hitler Youth. He also wears a
medical training merit emblem.

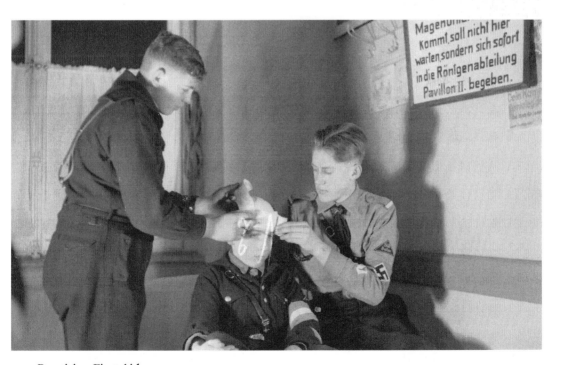

Practising First Aid
Two Hitler Youth, one's shoulder patch indicating the South Baden area, administer to a
comrade's head wound while signage reads 'Stomach or kidney complaints should not wait here,
but go straight to the Ronigen Department Pavilion II.'

'In remembrance of the KLV-Camp, Christmas 1942'

So reads the notation on the reverse of this photo, a section of a larger portrait of some some seventy-five boys, Hitler Youth attendants and the *Kinderlanverschikung* camp staff.

The KLV, or 'Sending Children to the Country' organisation, one of a myriad Third Reich social service programmes, was part of the national plan to evacuate children from metropolitan sites to the countryside. It served two purposes: firstly, to place them a safe distance from Allied bombing, and secondly to allow further control and indoctrination. Parents were dissuaded from visiting their children and those who attempted to keep them from the camps faced the stigma of being labeled 'unpatriotic'.

Raised by the Sword

Adult supervisors, instructors and officials gather at the entrance to a Hitler Youth camp.

'He who marches in the Hitler Youth is not one among millions, but a soldier of an idea.'

Baldur von Schirach, Reichs Youth Minister

Hitler Youth Box Office Hit

Published in December 1932 and written by K. A. Schenzinger, *Hitler Youth Quex* was made into a popular Third Reich film in 1933, the year of Hitler's ascendency to power. The plot involves a fifteen-year-old boy nicknamed 'Quex' who joins the Berlin Hitler youth in defiance of his commuist neighbourhood as well as of his father. In the end he pays for his loyalty to the Nazi Party with his life and becomes another of its martyrs. A quote from the novel sums up the mindset espoused by the party wherein a 'blood response' rather than analytical thought is held in highest esteem: 'The more he distanced himself from the camp, the faster he walked, diagonally across and through the forest toward the glow of the fire. Not for a moment did he reflect what he was doing there. It felt good during this night to march toward that light, and so he simply marched.'

With a title change to *Our Flag Leads Us Forward*, it was released in the US, which at the time was home to a large number of pro-Nazi fans of German descent. Eventually some 1 million viewed the film in Europe and the US.

Steel Wolfcubs

Hitler Youth training mirrored the Nazi emphasis on the physical over the intellectual, a paradigm impressed upon the secondary and university educational systems, resulting in a dramatic drop in the quality of the German student's knowledge base. Anti-intellectualism was a hallmark of the Third Reich's effort to produce soldier-citizens that 'felt' rather than thought, that obeyed rather than questioned.

Hitler Youth Camp – Leisnig, Germany

In March 1942 Hitler authorised the formation of special 'military competency camps', or *Wehrertuchtigungslager*, to prepare sixteen to eighteen year olds for combat, the act prompted by the attrition rate on the Eastern Front. Boys attended the training camps during school holidays, with 226 camps in operation by late 1943 and over 500,000 Hitler Youth taking part.

Hitler Youth boys were requied to serve as guards of captured Polish youth in special camps to hone their techniques of subjugation. Members of the Hitler Youth also served heroically as the rescuers of civilains trapped in burning buildings during the incessant aerial bombing raids of the later years of the war.

From Different Worlds
A mother who experienced the First World War
and its aftermath must now face the effects of the
Nazi State and its plans for her son. As he gazes
upwards, her gaze falls downward.

Cycle Soldiers in Training
While older Hitler Youth boys will soon grow into real uniforms, they retain their bicycles as
many German soldiers served in bicycle-mounted units as far afield as the Russian front. At home
Hitler Youth often patrolled in search of prohibited behaviour by their fellow young people,
often engaging in physical confrontations with non-Hitler Youth youths – some of whom had
formed their own organisations and were involved in anti-State 'rebellious' acts such as dancing
to American jazz music, which often saw them punished with prison terms or concentration
camp internment.

Motorised Hitler Youth
Dressed in their black winter uniforms,
Hitler Youth boys move up from bicycles to
motorcycles – one of the perks of membership and
for many more appealing than academic studies
or church services. Eventually some of the same
boys would be making a quantum leap to infantry
motorcycle units.

Hitler Youth Naval Divsion
Snapped in 1937, a young Hitler Youth *Kreigsmarine* cadet has offered a ride aboard his DKW
SB200 to a lady friend who has donned his cap. The registration plate indicates the location as
Westphalia in west central Germany.

Cowboy Fixation
A father and Hitler Youth son are apparently fans of cowboy movies, such Americana being popular in pre-war Germany, Tom Mix among them. Along with the huge Stetsons and revolver, the rustic log cabin lends a 'Wild West' backdrop.

A Third Reich Stamp Celebrates the Day of Youth Allegiance, 1943
A blonde-haired boy and girl of the Hitler Youth appeared in this stylised image of Aryan physical perfection. Nazi programmes appealed to German youth since it seemed to grant them status beyond their years, as well as well as encouraging a more 'liberal' attitude toward boy-girl physical relationships, the underlying motivation being securing control of children by the State over the family and also promoting a higher birth rate to increase the Third Reich's supply of military replacements.

Parade Rest
Siblings in matching poses have their
portraits taken on a cobblestone-lined
street. The girl wears lederhosen while
the two smaller boys wear the standard
summer Hitler Youth uniform of brown
shirt, black shorts and scarf. The older
boy appears out of uniform in a natty
sport coat and tie.

Military Family
With one son already in the Luftwaffe
and another in the Hitler Youth, a
German family poses for an apparently
highly processed professional portrait.

   Hitler Youth members offered a
pool of potential recruits for the Nazi
military and paramilitary organisations
including the SA, the SS, and the
Waffen-SS, which found the various
branches of the armed forces competing
for the best of the candidates, the
criteria being physical appearance,
sports achievements, leadership skills
and ideological correctness. Various
incentives and inducements were offered
to entice the best students, including
enrollment in special Hitler leadership
schools as well as financial subsidies to
the students' parents.

Two out of Three
A highly decorated officer, wearing his First World War decorations, and his wife pose with their two older sons, one a corporal, the other an officer, joined by their younger son still in short pants. After the attack on Poland, Hitler restricted the displaying of First World War medals as it was a war Germany had lost.

Following in their Bootsteps
Bookended between two Luftwaffe soldiers, what appears to be a Hitler Youth boy has stepped into a uniform tailored to his size. Windows in the background have been taped against bomb blasts, indicating a wartime timeframe.

Still Life

A mother and Hitler Youth son sit on fashionable rattan furniture and read together, separated by a solitary cactus – a rare and exotic plant in Germany at the time. A handwritten notation on the reverse reads 'Mother and son reading in the kitchen.'

The infamous Nazi-inspired nationwide frenzy of book burnings was ignited on 10 May 1933, barely six months after Hitler took office. German youth ransacked libraries, both public and private, and destroyed banned writings by Jewish, communist and anti-fascist writers, including Marx, Freud and German Nobel Prize winner Thomas Mann. Concurrently, Hitler's *Mein Kampf*, the blueprint of the Nazi dictatorship, had by the end of the war saw some 8 million copies printed in sixteen languages.

Who owns the copyright to *Mein Kampf*? Adolf Hitler, as its author, owned the exclusive rights to his book simply by writing it in 1925, but today the legal ownership is a matter of controversy. One claimant was Adolf's sister, Paula Wolf; another was the Bavarian Ministry of Finance (Hitler being an Austrian by birth), who in 1951 had being given the non-English rights by the Allies, and thereafter endeavored to limit its printing. German authorities support the notion that Adolf Hitler's copyright has been legally transferred to the Finance Ministry of the Free State of Bavaria as it opposes proliferation of the book. Various other countries continue to publish the book, including the US (first published as *My Battle* by Houghton Miflin in 1933), without any clear pronouncements as to where royalties are being paid, if at all.

However, it is known that the American government collected royalties on its sale for decades after the war. Houghton-Miflin earned revenues of several hundred thousand dollars, but eventually donated all the monies to charity after the appearance of a 2000 *US News and World Report* article brought the matter to public attention. Until 1999, *Mein Kampf* was the second-ranked bestseller on the German Amazon website. Both Amazon and Barnes & Noble, after protests, decided to block German sales. The book is currently available from both internet sites around the world.

ID in Transition

A Hitler Youth member has matriculated onto flight cadet status as indicated by his two identification photos chronicling the years of his membership.

Memories of War Past

Family members gathered to examine a photo album have become the subject of a photograph themselves. They sit around a table occupied by kitschy figures, including a ceramic miniature *pickelhaube* spiked First World War helmet. The two infantry soldiers, one showing the uniform insignia of an *Obergefreiter* (lance corporal), and both holding cigarettes are perhaps the uncles or older brothers of the young boy seated in the center. He has apparently donned one of their great coats and caps – too large for him for the present. Behind him, the framed portrait of a young First World War soldier with his Iron Cross Second Class ribbon is that of his father, now seen wearing a bow tie and sweater. For some reason, his wife has averted her eyes from the camera, perhaps examining a photograph.

In Command
In charge of four smaller boys, a group leader gives the camera a withering stare.

We all believe on this earth in Adolf Hitler, our leader.
We believe that National Socialism will be the only creed for our people.
We believe that there is a God in Heaven who created us, leads, and directs us.
And we believe that this God has sent us Adolf Hitler so that Germany should be a foundation stone in all eternity.

Words appearing on a Hitler Youth poster.

Formal Portrait of a Hitler Youth

To New Hieghts
Young *Flieger-HJ* members must first haul their glider up the hill from which it will take to the air. Training in similar craft was a precursor to joining the Luftwaffe and a means by which pre-war Germany could circumvent post-First World War restrictions on German rearmanent. The Olympic symbol on the glider indicates the year is 1936, during which the IOC games were held in Berlin.

Hitler Youth in Flight – Proto Luftwaffe Pilot
Now airborne and soaring over the hills, the young pilot sitting in an open frame must land the glider safely on its skidplate minus any landing wheels.

Martial Arts
Wearing the emblem of the *Deutsche Arbeitsfront* (German Labor Front), two boys take center ring in a boxing match attended by their fellow workers of all ages.

Martial sports like boxing were an integral part of training programmes at all levels of Hitler Youth, as well as during RAD service leading into military training. At one point the authorities had to throttle back on the intensity of the fisticuffs as the medical profession had noted a significant amount of injuries to both young children and older adults after taking up the sport.

By 1936 daily school sessions for physical training had increased from two to three periods; by 1938, it further was increased to five periods. Not only students, but teachers below fifty had to pass compulsory PT courses.

Constantly on the Move

An almost incessant round of marching, singing, hiking, maneuvers, sports competitions and rallies occupied the youth of Germany as part of an all-pervasive conditioning process to produce unconditionally obedient soldiers. Many German military as well as Hitler Youth songs contained virulently anti-Semitic lyrics, a popular Hitler Youth example containing the following: 'Yes, when the Jewish blood splashes from the knives, things will go twice as well.'

Senior Student

As Reich Youth leader, von Schirach opened special *Adolf-Hitler Schulen* in an effort to create an organisation competing with the standard German school system. However, instruction was inferior, with most academic study replaced by sports and physical training – again, the complete submergence of the individual to the State as the prime directive for producing a generation of obedient warriors.

Focus on National Socialism
A Hitler Youth member has arrived at one of the special elite schools, in this case a *Reiterschule* or a training facility for horsemanship, as indicated by the handwritten notations on the reverse of this out-of-focus image.

Olympian Heights
A Hitler Youth squad, having brought their banner to their rooftop vantage, pauses for a group photo. As highly indoctrinated 'true believers', many would join elite units and fight with a fanaticism and viciousness that often surpassed older troops.

Students of the Gun
Their small-bore rifles stacked military fashion, a squad of Hitler Youth record a day at camp. Those who eventually joined the SS Division *Hitler-Jugend* would see combat during the Allied landings at Normandy in June 1944, some manning tanks and fighting with distinction.

The Face of a Fierce Future
Hitler Youth members, the future leaders of the Thousand-Year Reich, though still teenagers, emulate Hitler's call to the youth of Germany to be 'as fast as a greyhound, tough as leather and hard as Krupp steel.'

All in Step

In 1945, during the last months of the Third Reich, fifteen year olds were conscripted into the military. But as early as 1943 entire school classes of students aged fifteen to seventeen years old were drafted into anti-aircraft defence units. Hitler Youth boys put up fanatical resistance in the last weeks of the war as Allied forces entered Germany. They were also encountered murdering prisoners when concentration camps were being liberated.

Father and Son Studio Portrait

Even in this non-color photo, blue eyes are apparent, a sign of 'Aryan racial perfection' as delineated by Nazi racial doctrine. The photo, taken at the Max Struve studio in Hamburg, was produced as a mailable postcard for distribution by the family.

Brother and Sister – *Junge Madel* and *Hitler-Jugend*

In Precise Procession
Older Hitler Youth members marching in review are saluted by members of the regular army and a black-uniformed Hitler Youth official while a number of BdM girls appraise the boys.

Strange Instrument
Hitler Youth member and musician Gunter Rofsmann holds an unusual tri-horned brass instrument, the flugelhorn, and wears the black 'swallow's nest' shoulder insignia of a musician. As part of the Nazi indoctrination programme, Hitler Youth training included instruction in both voice and musical instruments, eventually forming hundreds of music groups performing at local Hitler Youth events, celebrations for Nazi officials, and even touring on the Russian front.

Potted Plants and Portrait within a Portrait
Wearing his official tracksuit and seated in an exotic bamboo and wicker chair, a Hitler Youth elite member has autographed his photo.

Streifendienst (SRD) – *Hitler-Jugend* Security Officer

A Nazi Party membership pin and a cuff title identify a member of the special group of Hitler Youth males aged sixteen to eighteen who worked closely with the Gestapo and SS units. Their duties included policing their fellow youth who had transgressed in some fashion against Hitler Youth behavioural policies. They were also charged with hunting out non-Hitler Youth German youths guilty of 'suspicious' acts. As it were, the *Streifendienst* were SS and Gestapo-in-training. The boys were culled from the most fanatical Hitler Youth and prepared for later duties dealing with inferior races, including the killing of civilians.

Hitler Youth Leader and Fans

A bicycle-mounted group leader is observed by two civilian boys while a soldier pedals along the cobblestone street in the background. The boy may have attended one of the thirty-nine *Nationalpolitische Erziehungsanstalten* (Napolas), the special schools for elite Hitler Youth training operated by the SS with the intent of moulding new Nazi Party and military leaders. Emphasis included boxing, war games, rowing, sailing, gliding, shooting and riding motorcycles.

Hitler Youth Christmas Songfest
Caught by the camera with a variety of expressions, boys of the Hitler Youth and girls of the BdM and RAD gather for a holiday celebration. One RAD member appears to be gazing heavenward. Note the paper worn beneath shoes, apparently to prevent marring the floor.

Mutual Attraction
Teenage BdM girls and Hitler Youth boys greet each other at the train station. The Nazi State, intent on producing an endless supply of warriors, placed no sanctions on births out of wedlock, and in fact often encouraged it.

Stamp of Approval

One of a series of Third Reich stamps in praise of the young members of the Reichs Labor Service (*Reichsarbeitdienst*) or RAD. A compulsory paramilitary organisation established by law in June 1934, the service saw nineteen to twenty-five year olds, male and female, working in the fields with farmers or performing other labour for a period of six months within a military disciplined programme. During this time the boys drilled as soldiers but carried spades.

'Grinder Express'

Having inscribed their team nickname on the transport cart, a team of RAD boys pause from their heavy labours.

Stand-in for a Rifle
A RAD officer, holding his handbook, gives instruction in the proper holding of the shovel when 'presenting arms'.

Teenagers in Training
As part of Hitler's plan to resolve Germany's massive unemployment problems, the RAD provided cheap labour, indoctrinated the young and also served to sidestep the restrictions of the post-First World War Versailles Treaty, which sought to limit German military expansion. Morevover, the RAD provided a means to transition German youth into a military mould for later incorporation into the various branches of the Wehrmacht.

Proud RAD Father
Wearing his Nazi Party pin and what
appears to be a Winter Relief 'tinnie'
badge, indicating he contributed to the
annual donation campaign, a father
poses with his son in RAD uniform. His
daughter is also of age for RAD service.
The boy, belt in hand, has treated his
uniform casually and smokes a cigarette,
which Nazi social planners railed against
as a health hazard. His actions may thus
indicate teenage rebelliousness.

RAD Boy in Full Kit
RAD recruits came in all sizes and from
all social classes and entered a regimen
that emphasised 'classlessness', all
members being ostensbily graded on
performance rather than socio-economic
status or level of education.

'Spade Soldier'
A closer look reveals his cap's
RAD insignia – a swastika within
a spade.

No Exemptions

Uniformity of Illusion

Endless Uniformity

More Power
A RAD youth has moved up to a larger motorcycle, in this case a civilian model DKW most likely 'requisitioned' for military usage as the war grew.

Olympian Heights
A young RAD man poses for the camera, his mother and friends by his side. As the superior race they were firm in their conviction that they would be the masters of the new Pan-European State

Marching Under a New Banner
RAD members parade during a graduation ceremony.

Metamorphosis
A camera records the transformation of RAD youth into an SA man.

Next Step of a New Recruit, Autumn 1936
A nattily dressed young man has just arrived for
military service, much to the amusement of the NCOs
greeting him. Compulsory military conscription was
re-established in 1936 as Germany re-armed at a
blitzkrieg pace in violation of the Versailles Treaty.

Describing the kind of boy the Hitler Youth *didn't*
want, a magazine article published in 1937 featured
a photo of well-dressed boy in suit and tie with the
caption: 'This is the type we hate — the pint-sized
grownup in a Manchester suit, collar, and tie, with a
white handkerchief in the breast pocket, dressed to the
nines — a delight to his aunts. We prefer a real boy.'

On Parade
BdM (*Bund Deutsches Madchen*) girls wearing their uniforms and marching in unison are
joined by a girl in civilian clothing, perhaps set outside the group for the infraction. They have
apparently paraded under the window of someone with a camera. Some of the girls have spotted
their observer and glance in his or her direction.

One Voice

Accompanied by an accordion, BdM girls sing as they march. Many young German girls and women literally fell under Hitler's spell, overcome with an ecstatic devotion of fanatical intensity. Also possessed of a particular virulent hatred of Jews, the German mothers passed this trait onto their daughters, who in turn responded fervently to the anti-Semitic rhetoric of the BdM indocrination. A popular BdM song, one of many with similar virulent lyrics, went as follows:

> We've given up the Christian line,
> For Christ was just a Jewish swine,
> As for his Mother – what a shame –
> Cohn was the lady's real name.

Child of the Times

A young girl wears an overseas cap and a leather belt as a sash and carries a dress dagger plus the added touch of a pipe – all likely borrowed from a family member in the military.

Lehre dein Kind:

Lehre dein Kind, alles Lebende zu schützen!

Lehre dein Kind, die Schönheit der Natur zu sehen!

Lehre dein Kind, daß die Tiere Mitbewohner dieser Welt sind, und daß wir kein Recht haben, ihnen Fallen zu stellen und sie von der Erde auszurotten!

Lehre dein Kind, daß derjenige, der sich mit Tieren nicht zu befreunden weiß und keine Kameradschaft mit Hund, Katze, Pferd oder sonstigen Geschöpfen im Pelz- oder Federkleid findet, nie die richtige Lebensfreude haben kann, und sei er auch noch so reich, in Wirklichkeit sich seelisch arm fühlen wird!

Lehre dein Kind, nie nutzlos zu töten und nie zum Zeitvertreib Tiere zu verletzen, zu verstümmeln oder zu zerstören.

Lehre dein Kind, daß ein gefangenes und angekettetes Tier nicht weniger leidet, als ein menschliches Wesen!

Lehre dein Kind, daß, wer für sich Mitleid und Sympathie verlangt, dies auch jedem andern Lebewesen zubilligen muß!

Aus „Das Tier", Verlag Dr. Höhne — Ulm a. D

Lehre Dein Kind – 'Teach Your Children' Kindness to All Creatures

The Nazi social planners called for an enlightened treatment of animals. Stiff penalties were meted out to those guilty of abusing nonhuman creatures. The commercial postcard sums up the mindset with no small amount of irony. Excerpts from the poem include:

Teach your child to protect all living things.

Teach your child to see the beauty of nature.

Teach your child that anmals are cohabitants of this world and that we have no right to set traps for them or to eradicate them from the earth.

Teach your child never to kill needlessly and never to injure, mutilate or destroy animals as a pastime.

Teach your child that those who desire compassion and sympathy for themselves must also accord this to every other living creature.

Properly Attired Hitler Youth

'For Sale'
Young BdM nembers attending
a rally pose under a portion of a
banner with ironic wording.

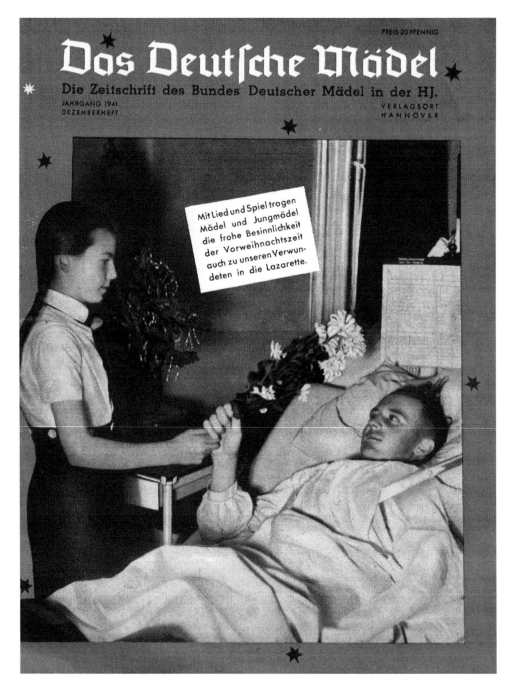

PREIS 20PFENNIG

Das Deutsche Mädel

Die Zeitschrift des Bundes Deutscher Mädel in der HJ.

JAHRGANG 1941
DEZEMBERHEFT

VERLAGSORT
HANNOVER

Mit Lied und Spiel tragen Mädel und Jungmädel die frohe Besinnlichkeit der Vorweihnachtszeit auch zu unseren Verwundeten in die Lazarette.

Casualties Mount from the Eastern Front, December 1941
The cover of the official magazine for the Federation of German Girls features a young member bringing flowers to a bedridden soldier. The text of the insert reads: 'With song and play, young women and young girls carry the glad tidings of Christmas Eve to our wounded in military hospitals.' The young soldier's left arm seems to be held in some form of traction, with the outline of a cast visible beneath the sheets. The magazine issue date coincides with the Japanese attack on the US naval base at Pearl Harbor, Hawaii, and America's declaration of war against Japan. As part of the Tripartite Pact, Hitler in turn declares war against the US.

Domestication

BdM girls are lined up to show their talents at cleaning and polishing men's boots. Working with one's hands was considered mandatory of a true German girl and evidence she understood the 'blood and soil' philosophy of the NSDAP. Hundreds of thousands of young girls toiled on farms or provided household aid – often thirteen hours a day six days a week – as part of the RAD service. They were also charged with collecting medicinal herbs and teas, some 6.5 million hours being invested by a million BdM girls in that endeavor. Later the mandatory work programmes continued in war industry factories, women replacing men sent to the front.

BdM Girls Dance in the Snow

Dressed in their waitress uniforms, several girls are apparently unaffected by the cold weather. As part of their national labour service, the girls of the *Bund deutscher Madel* were required to work as helpers for the wives of farmers, the rapport between the city dwellers and the rural inhabitants often lacking. The farmers accused them of being lazy or sexually promiscuous with soldiers, while the latter considered the farmers as abusive and exploitative, both points of conjecture often valid.

Warmer Attire
Now bundled up aginst the wintry temperature, BdM girls enjoy the company of one of their number's children.

Older BdM Girls in RAD Uniform
Only two of the thirty-nine elite SS Napola schools were designated for the training of girls, Nazi positions of leadership and power being reserved for males.

BdM Girls and RAD Boys Socialise

While women were regarded as non-combatants to be shielded from the harshness of war, a number volunteered as *SS-Helferinnen*, SS Female Helpers. Some took their training at the women's concentration camp at Ravensbruck, where they observed the cruel actions of the male guards upon the prisoners. They often took part in promiscuous sex with the guards along with full participation in the severe military discipline, all designed to separate them from conventional morality and codes of conduct and enabling them in turn to often outstrip their male counterparts in violence and cruelty.

Not on Equal Footing

An SA man greets a troop of BdM girls, who return his salute. A camera stands ready on its tripod to record the event.

Glaube und Schonheit – Faith
and Beauty
A Third Reich commercial postcard extolling
the role of BdM girls, many of whom
went on to serve on anti-aircraft crews in
the last days of the war. Braided hair was
much encouraged by the BdM leaders as a
preferred *Volkish* look.

Model BdM

Planning for the Future
Third Reich social engineers
sought to produce the superior
German woman/breeder; for
example, via the *Hohen Frauen*
or 'High Women' taking part in
the '*Glaube und Schonheit*' or
Faith and Beauty Programme that
sought the most attractive girls of
above-average intelligence who
were then instructed in gymnastics,
horseback riding, pistol shooting,
fencing and automobile driving.
The concept was one developed
by chief Third Reich architect
Albert Speer, Youth Leader Baldur
von Schirach and filmmaker Leni
Riefenstahl, three of the Third
Reich's 'beautiful people'.

Assigned to the Butcher's Shop

BdM Girl from Austria

The girl wears the brown 'climbing jacket' or *Kletterjacke*, a popular BdM wardrobe item, along with the standard white shirt and black scarf.

German children joined forces with the SS and the police battalions to forcibly evict Polish and Czech peasants from their homes in order to create *lebensraum* for ethnic Germans to repopulate. A German female student after watching the SS evict Polish villagers wrote in 1942: 'Sympathy with these creatures? No, at most I felt quietly appalled that such people exist, people who are in their very being so infinitely alien and incomprehensible to us that there is no way to reach them. For the first time in our lives, people whose life or death is a matter of indifference.'

Child Soldiers

Wearing early style M18 helmets, two very young soldiers appear to regard the camera with opposite emotions in this pre-war photo.

Boys Manning AA Gun
Guarding a factory and power plant, a team of Hitler Youth boys operate a mobile 88 mm cannon. Girls also served on gun teams. In the last months of the war, as bombs rained down upon the German cities, the young anti-aircraft crews often manned their guns to the death.

'In Recollection of Our Wedding – from Ingeborg and Walter'
As the photo postcard was being penned on 20 March 1943, the recent Stalingrad disaster has staggered the German public. The children, though too young for the Hitler Youth, would have been caught in the midst of the increasingly intense aerial bombing of Nazi Germany, their names and fate unknown.

Betet Brüder, daß mein und euer Opfer
Gott wohlgefalle.

Flieger

Clemens Mayr

geb. am 16. Nov. 1927 in München

gefallen am 30. April 1945
bei Canov in Mecklenburg

'Flyer'

The parents of seventeen-year-old Clemens Mayr of Munich have used a childhood photo for his memorial card, the boy dying in northern Germany a week before the war ended. There are no images of swastikas or words of a 'hero's death' as seen on earlier war years memorial cards. Young boys such as Clemens were given a few days' worth of training and sent up in the last of Nazi Germany's aircraft to face the Allies commanding the skies.

Nicht wir allein, die um dich weinen
Nein, wer dich gekannt der liebte dich,
Der Herr er kennt und liebt die feinen
Drum nahm er dich fo früh zu sich.

Death Card for a Child Soldier

Alois Schiesl's face appears on his *sterbebild* (memorial or 'death card'), which was sent out by his relatives to announce his death on 11 November 1944 at the age of 'nineteen and five months following a serious wound'. He was buried in a 'hero's cemetery' in Saargemund, a German town in the Alsace-Lorraine. Apparently no current photo of the soldier was available so a uniform was sketched around a much younger boy.

Saargemund is located in the Saar River basin in north-east France at the German border. The region of Alsace-Lorraine had been removed from German control as the result of the First World War but in 1940 was re-incorporated into the Reich, which then initiated the process of Germanising the population, part of whom spoke German and considered themselves German while the French speakers thought themselves French.

Home Front Casualties, February 1944

On the night of 25/26 February 1944, Maria Johanna Windolz, aged thirty-seven, Josef, eight, and Maria, three, were killed during a 'terror bombing' of the city of Augsburg. The combined Allied raid was the final of a series termed 'The Big Week', the city being targeted as the location of a Messerschmidt aircraft factory. During the daylight hours the American Eighth Air Force bombed on 25 February, followed by the RAF, with a total of some 594 under Bomber Command coordination destroying large parts of the city center. Minus 18-degree temperatures froze the fire hydrants, making it difficult to put out the over 1,000 fires. The last bombings killed 730 people, among them the mother and her two children. The memorial card carried the words of the husband and father: 'Mein liebe und meinen lieben kinderlein' – 'my love and my beloved children.'

Bühler, Bobingen

Farewell to a Father and Husband

His sister waiting her turn, a young boy follows his mother to bid their final farewells during the funeral for a high-ranking officer. Thousands more such funerals would follow across Germany and Austria as the war's attrition ground on. Hundreds of thousands more of the dead would remain buried in graves across the Soviet Union as the German forces lost ground, retreating back to their homeland. Many of those Eastern European cemeteries were obliterated when Red Army forces came upon them, the bodies never being returned. Post-war efforts to recover the dead continue.

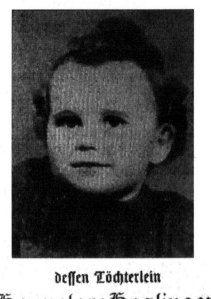

Stabsgefreiter

Josef Haslinger

geboren am 15. Oktober 1917 in
Passau-Auerbach
gefallen am 26. Dezember 1944 in
Mazbites (Kurland)

dessen Töchterlein

Hannelore Haslinger

geboren am 27. Juni 1941
durch Terrorangriff
gefallen am 29. Dezember 1944

Father and Daughter, Christmas 1944

Josef Haslinger's death card states he died at age twenty-seven on the day after Christmas, 26 December 1944, in Kurland (Courland), the Latvian Baltic peninsula where by mid-October some 500,000 German and 20,000 Latvian Waffen-SS troops had been trapped by Soviet forces. Although some were able to escape from the encirclement, the remaining Germans and Latvians managed to hold the front against several major Russian offensives until the war ended on 8 May 1945, one of the last German surrenders of the Second World War. According to German estimates, Soviet Army losses included 390,000 dead, wounded or POW, and as well as 2,388 tanks, 659 planes, 900 cannons, and 1,440 machine guns. By 23 May, two weeks after the war ended, some 180,000 German troops surrendered to Soviet captivity. Those Latvian Legion soldiers who had fought as allies of the Germans were shot as Soviet traitors.

Three days after her father had been killed, Hannelore Haslinger, aged three and a half, died during an Allied bombing raid.

Opposite above: **Postscript Photo**

The handwriting, in German, on the reverse of this photo, translates to 'For our big brother from your family – Siegmund and Mutter'. The same person has then written 'Berlin, Germany, 4 Nov. 1945' in English. As the war in Europe had been over since 8 May 1945, it is possible the family has sent the photo to the older uniformed boy, then in a British or American POW camp. In the photo he wears a Luftwaffe cadet uniform. The eventual fate of the family is unknown. While tens of thousands of German POWs died in Soviet captivity, strong evidence indicates that thousands of German POWs also died in Allied prison camps due to starvation and exposure – a long-kept secret. In comparision, millions of Soviet POWs died after German capture.

Last Minute Soldiers of the Third Reich, 21 October 1944
The US Signal Corp Radio press release photo carried the following caption: 'Three small German boys were picked up on a road near Aachen for firing on advancing American soldiers. From left are Willy Eischenburg, 14, a Hitler Youth; his brother, Bernard, 10; Hubert Heinrichs, 10, and another Eischenburg Brother Victor, 8.' (No final disposition of the boys' fate was included.)

The photo was dated to the last day of the Aachen battle, which had begun on 14 October, and is noted as the first German city to be captured after American troops entered Nazi Germany. Hitler had commanded the city not fall as it was the capital of Charlemagne, the founder of the First Reich, and thus Nazi 'holy ground'. The Germans waged a fierce and effective house-to-house defence against superior odds, but the American air power and artillery subdued the German tanks and defenders, most of the city being destroyed in the process. American losses counted nearly 3,200 casualties, while the Germans lost some 5,000. While most of the civilian population, some 165,000, had evacuated, a purported 40,000 had remained as they considered the Americans as liberators.

The Fog of War – US Signal Corp Photo, 14 March 1945
As the last weeks of war still raged in Germany, civilian women of all ages were fortunate to receive evacuation aid from US forces, thereby not being subjected to Red Army revenge that included the mass rape of hundreds of thousands of females of all ages.

The photo, taken by First Lieutenant John D. Moors, is stamped on the reverse side with the location – the city of Schaffhausen in Germany. However, it may be in error as Schaffausen was actually in neutral Swiss territory. The year previously, on 1 April 1944, a formation of fifty US B-24 Liberators accidentally bombed Schaffausen rather than their designated target of Ludwigshafen am Rhein some 235 km north. The latter is situated on the right bank (north side) of the Rhine River, thereby mistakenly assumed to be the German city. Some forty fatalities, numerous injuries, and property damage resulted from the error attributed to bad weather. By October 1944, $4 million had been paid to the Swiss in restitution.

Final Total

Hundreds of thousands of German children growing up during 1933–45 saw their fathers only during infrequent furloughs. Others born near the end of the war were never to meet them, with more than a million soldiers dying in the last twelve months of the Third Reich. Hitler in his Berlin bunker hideout, finally admitting the war was lost, railed against the people he led to war, saying that since they were not victorious, they had no right to exist. He called for the total self-destruction of Germany's remaining infrastructure but his wishes were not carried out. Only when Berlin was completely overrun by Soviet forces and Hitler had committed suicide did the German high command surrender unconditionally on 8 May 1945. The fate of the country was to remain divided for more than half a century, and the fate of the children seen here remains unknown.